HISTORICAL SCHOLARSHIP
&
HISTORICAL THOUGHT

AN INAUGURAL LECTURE
DELIVERED AT CAMBRIDGE ON
16 MAY 1944

BY

G. N. CLARK
Regius Professor of Modern History

T0349129

CAMBRIDGE
AT THE UNIVERSITY PRESS
1944

CAMBRIDGE
UNIVERSITY PRESS

University Printing House, Cambridge CB2 8BS, United Kingdom

Published in the United States of America by Cambridge University Press, New York

Cambridge University Press is part of the University of Cambridge.

It furthers the University's mission by disseminating knowledge in the pursuit of education, learning and research at the highest international levels of excellence.

www.cambridge.org
Information on this title: www.cambridge.org/9781107682900

© Cambridge University Press 1944

This publication is in copyright. Subject to statutory exception and to the provisions of relevant collective licensing agreements, no reproduction of any part may take place without the written permission of Cambridge University Press.

First published 1944
Re-issued 2014

A catalogue record for this publication is available from the British Library

ISBN 978-1-107-68290-0 Paperback

Cambridge University Press has no responsibility for the persistence or accuracy of URLs for external or third-party internet websites referred to in this publication, and does not guarantee that any content on such websites is, or will remain, accurate or appropriate.

HISTORICAL SCHOLARSHIP AND HISTORICAL THOUGHT

THE SHARE which historians contribute to the common stock of ideas and beliefs varies greatly from time to time and from place to place. Although it can never be estimated exactly, we may safely say that in this country for many generations past it has never been a negligible proportion. Of late it has grown more important, most of all during the present war. In any disturbed and violent time men wish to know how things have come to be as they are; and in our time there is a further reason for historical curiosity. All of us, whether in the services, or in civilian war work, in the universities, or in our homes, have come into contact with foreigners, allies or refugees, from many countries; we have learnt how they are inspired by historical memories and how their mental habits are derived from their national histories. As the distant continents have closed in upon our island, so the centuries too have closed in. We discuss the present and the future with new friends whose national experience diverged from our own perhaps in the eighteenth century, or at the Reformation or in the Middle Ages, or even with some who have no part in the inheritance of Greece and Rome. In trying to understand their problems and their points of view we have discovered afresh how much of the

3

past is still alive in their minds and ours. There is no longer any need for historians to attract attention by their once familiar devices of making some distant age appear astonishingly like our own or, alternatively, of making the recent past, say the Victorian age, seem quaintly different and remote. Perhaps there has never been a time when so many people seriously tried to understand the world around them, or when so many tried to understand it in the light of history.

Not only does the reading and talking public enquire into many historical questions: the state also sets many people to work at history. The practice, to be sure, is not entirely new. More than two hundred and fifty years ago Thomas Rymer of Sidney Sussex College was appointed, mainly at the instance of Charles Montagu of Trinity, to edit the great folio volumes of his *Foedera* which we still use. On these there have followed series upon series of official publications of documents, far too expensive for any authority other than the state to finance, providing the chief materials for the study of our history. Some of them have dealt with very recent transactions, like the *British Diplomatic Documents* in which two eminent Cambridge scholars, Dr Gooch and the late Master of Peterhouse, set a memorable example of 'objectivity' and method; but taken together they cover every period from the very earliest. Nor has the state been content only to publish materials and the subsidiary apparatus of catalogues, calendars and indexes. It has employed historians to write accounts of events and institutions of many kinds, and if, in this country, the only examples of such work on a large scale are the official histories of recent wars, it is nevertheless true that an extensive and varied historical library may be extracted from the blue books of the last hundred years.

During the present war the demand both for historical materials and for applied history has become greater than ever before. The publication of recent diplomatic documents is to continue. A numerous and well-organized staff is already preparing narratives of the work of the civil departments during the war. Official history, composed from a limited class of materials and necessarily to some degree subject to censorship, seems to be intermediate between historical writing in the full sense and the editing of historical materials. As to its usefulness even for current purposes of the war there seems to be general agreement, and it is also clear that it is work for which a regular historical training is a good preparation. Several of our most distinguished historians, again, are employed in other kinds of research work for government departments. Indeed, when we think of all the invitations which are addressed to historians by official and by semi-official bodies, we may well grumble 'Et spes et ratio studiorum in Caesare tantum'. But, in this matter, as in its relations with the universities, the state in this country knows how to respect the independence of enquiry. It does not ask the historians to depart from their academic standards. For its own information it requires the truth uncoloured by any preference for one policy over another. Even when historians are engaged not in informing government departments but in propaganda, their training enables them to maintain the high traditions of that honest advocacy which a good cause deserves. Indeed, the greatest service which the historical faculties of the universities have rendered to the nation during the war is not that of the historians but that of the many hundreds of men and women who are able to serve the better in many spheres and at every level by virtue of their liberal education in historical studies.

Some of the qualities which we try to impart can no doubt be acquired equally well in other subjects. There is a prosaic intellectual efficiency which any good university training ought to improve: it consists in such obviously desirable qualities as accuracy, lucidity, a sense of relevance, the power of telling a good argument from a bad one, the power, so constantly needed in the age of the telephone and the shorthand-typist, of extracting the essentials from a mass of information. Liberal education is much more than that; but for the moment, as we are thinking of our effort in the war, it is enough to remember this, its utilitarian side. On this humdrum basis we build the education of the free man, that is, education for responsibility and especially for positions of intellectual responsibility, in which we have to make up our own minds and influence those of other people. There is a sufficient reason why history has become in modern times one of the subjects through which such a training is most commonly given. In a world like ours, which carries so much of the complex past along

6

with it, many kinds of administration, both in public affairs and in ordinary private business, require some knowledge of political or social or economic history. We give to undergraduates a three years' training—perhaps it is too short—not only in the ascertained results of historical research, but also in historical criticism. They learn how these results are arrived at; they learn that the primary moral virtue of truthfulness needs to be combined with skill in ascertaining what is true. When we look at the work which those whom we have trained are doing in the war, we become aware of some defects in our curricula and our examinations; we discuss among ourselves proposals for improving them in one way or another; but I believe we should all agree on the main point, that our history schools can regard the results of their work with satisfaction, and even with sober pride.

Is it not somewhat disquieting, then, that almost all the higher organization of historical studies is out of action or at best continues on a 'care and maintenance' footing? The publications of the Public Record Office and the Historical Manuscripts Commission are suspended; university research is almost at a standstill; undergraduates in our faculties are few in numbers; little provision is made for the future need of teachers of our subject in universities and schools. We grudge nothing to the service of the state, and we do not doubt that the state has needed all that it has taken; but, in the interests of the state itself, we are entitled to ask whether historical studies are at the present moment sufficiently valued. Already the supply of trained historians is inadequate to the official demand; the same is true of men and women who have received a general education in our historical schools. We cannot complain if a unique emergency restricts our academic life; but the emergency has lasted long: in the two wars some of our mature historians have spent nine years away from their special studies. When we plan for the return of peace in the future we must boldly ask for the approval we have earned and for the large sums of money which will be needed to bring our whole machinery back into full working trim.

Indeed, we ought to increase the range of our studies to cover still more countries and subjects. Here in Cambridge the munificence of the University Press has already made provision for American history, and there are other regions, such as the Slavonic lands, the Far East and Latin America, which we shall evidently need to study in the future more closely than hitherto. We shall also need more specialized guidance in various aspects of history nearer home, such as the fine arts; and these needs will continue to expand. Music, for instance, has become of late so significant a part of English life, that it may soon claim a place in our historical studies. If I look forward to such an increase in the number of our historical specialists, I have, let me hasten to add, no desire that the work of undergraduates should be more intensely specialized than it is already. On the contrary, if I may speak for myself, I should like to see undergraduates, and not only undergraduates but my own contemporaries as well, less exclusively absorbed in the study of monographs and periodicals than some of them appear to be, and more at leisure to read the great classics of historical and other writing, which have more durable merits than that of being up-to-date. Yet historical knowledge, like our knowledge of the natural sciences, is built up by specialists, who perpetually revise and correct the details of accepted conclusions. We must initiate the undergraduate into their methods, and we must not allow him to suppose that important results can be obtained by airy generalization or uncritical dogmatism.

Partly for this reason the historical schools in our universities have never paid much attention to a kind of history which is one of the most popular with the general reading public, the books of outlines or philosophical history which trace the fortunes of civilizations through hundreds or even thousands of years. The one standing joke against the historian is that if you ask him a question he says 'That is not in my period', and it seems reasonable to think poorly of him if his knowledge of his period is not set in a framework of universal history. We ought, however, first to be sure that we are not asking him to do more than can be fairly expected.

Some historians, and far more people who are not historians, believe that there is a general process of history which explains all its parts. This belief takes many forms. One form is the belief in progress, the belief that in spite of complications and set-backs, Man throughout his existence has been moving from bad to better and will finally attain to some good or best. The idea of progress, in all

9

its variations from the eighteenth-century faith in human perfectibility onwards, has been most popular when the final happy outcome appeared tolerably near at hand: it arose among men who felt that their own age was exceptional and had put the past behind it. The cruel turn of events in our generation has thrown many people back on an earlier type of belief in a general process of history, that which rejects progress and traces cycles of growth and decay. Much learning and much ingenuity have been devoted lately to explaining the mechanism of these cycles or to explaining that they work not by any mechanism but by a living principle. All these doctrines, whether of progress, of cycles, and yet others which profess only to reveal the laws of change, have this in common: they maintain that history taken as a whole has a plot. They imply that once you grasp the plot, you will be able to find the point of everything that happens to the world. The historical world, they tell us, is a planned world; the historical process (which nowadays usually includes the evolution of non-human nature) explains itself. There is nothing outside it that we need to apprehend in order to explain it.

There are many good reasons why working academic historians should distrust these ready-made keys to all historical problems. In their daily work of research they have to assume that each present moment, instead of being predetermined by everything that has already happened, is genuinely new. If the future is undetermined, history is not a whole; it is perpetually unfinished and there is no coherent whole consisting of past, present and future. For my own part I do not believe that any future consummation could make sense of all the irrationalities of the preceding ages. If it could not explain, still less could it justify. The crimes and sufferings of countless millions of human beings for a quarter of a million—or is it half a million?—years were facts as real as anything that can occur in the future in the same historical process. The future cannot undo them, and any one of them by itself frustrates the search for rationality in the world of time. To me, therefore, it seems that no historical investigation can provide either a philosophy, or a religion, or a substitute for religion, or even an adequate excuse for doing without a religion.

If in this I express only a personal opinion, I think I should have a general consensus of the working historians with me if I confined myself to the simpler conclusion that we work with limited aims. We try to find the truth about this or that, not about things in general. Our work is not to see life steadily and see it whole, but to see one particular portion of life right side up and in true perspective. The portion may be very large or very small. It may be confined to the history of one village; it may extend to the history of one country, perhaps to the history of one civilization. To the historian these differences of size do not look the same as they do to most people, because for him, as the French say, every thing has something of everything in it: he writes about the village as part of a county and of a diocese, as influenced by what goes on in distant continents; he writes about one century as following after, and in a sense conditioned by, all the others. But he would be a very bad historian if he tried to cram the history of the whole world, or even of the next village, into his village history. He has a subject, definite in time and place, even if, like many subjects in the history of thought and even of action, it seems to reach out to all the confines of knowledge. The historian's aims are limited by the succession of times and by positions in space.

In practice, of course, we always have to decide as we go along how to define our subjects and on what scale to treat them so as to avoid superficiality on the one hand and narrowness on the other. From the technical and from the literary point of view the historian's success or failure depends on innumerable decisions to include this and exclude that, which taken together constitute his selection of what he is to say. Even for the quickest and most confident worker it is often extremely difficult to decide whether to include or reject a particular fact. We have devices for evading the difficulty, for instance footnotes and appendices, to which we can relegate information which we wish to keep but cannot entirely assimilate into the body of our work. These expedients, however, never do away with the difficulty altogether even in small matters; and it sometimes meets us in very large matters when we have to decide whether to follow up some line of enquiry or to leave it to other workers. Now here we ought as far as possible to decide not by some mechanical rule of thumb, but by a really constructive judgment. Sometimes we must submit to a merely negative rule: for instance, a point comes when we have to drop an enquiry because we cannot go further without mastering a fresh foreign language, and for each of us there is some limit to the number of languages we can attempt. But it may happen that we make a negative rule for ourselves when it corresponds neither to our own natural limitations nor to the structure of our subject-matter.

I think the commonest example is seen when historians try to turn chronological periods into mutually exclusive subjects. Medieval studies have suffered when students of the Middle Ages have felt themselves absolved from reading classical authors or even debarred from reading them; after all, Aristotle and Vergil were more influential in the Middle Ages than all the clerks in all the chanceries of Christendom. It is not, however, medieval studies but those of some later periods, and above all of the most recent, that have been most impoverished by being treated in isolation. We cannot all study everything; we cannot, even with the most ingenious short cuts, study everything that is relevant to our work; but our principle of selection should always be to choose the more relevant and omit the less, not to apply a mechanical criterion like that of date.

Our greatest difficulties in defining the limits of ordinary historical work do not, however, arise from the differences of scale or differences between periods, or from the need to read more foreign languages than most of us find easy or convenient; they are those which involve the relation of history to other branches of study. We recognize that every history is the history of something, and, whatever that thing may be, there will probably be some other way of studying it besides the historical way. If we are to work satisfactorily at economic history we need at least some grasp of theoretical economics; for political and constitutional history, as Seeley taught us once and for all, we need political science, for imperial history some special knowledge of conditions and problems overseas; ecclesiastical history cannot be divorced from theology. The University has therefore special chairs for all these branches of history. Nor can we see any end to the new specialisms which may develop. For instance, there are already economic historians who study the questions of population with a technique so specialized that it may be called a historical branch of social biology. Again, it will not be long before the psychologists begin to provide historians with something more than the scraps of terminology and the occasional ornamental hints with which some of them enliven their accounts of human character and motive. As these specialisms multiply they become more technical. Historians of late have increasingly used statistical technique, sometimes applying it experimentally to intractable materials, but often gaining very valuable results. Until recently few historians did more than try to recover what was known or felt by the actors in the past; but now many of them work out interpretations which belong essentially to our own novel intellectual outlook. To take the simplest example, economic historians now interpret the thirteenth century and even the neolithic age in terms of net social output, investment, and so forth which no one in those centuries could possibly have understood.

All this, so long as it is well done, is excellent. It means that historians are making their due contribution to the general work of social and humane studies, and it is in accordance with the now familiar doctrine that ultimately there is no logical distinction between history and these studies. The more highly each special branch of history develops its appropriate method, the better results we may expect from what Maitland called 'the study of inter-dependences'. I may illustrate this from the instance of the history of science. This is not a new study, but until recently it often seemed both to historians and to scientists to be a secondary and outlying subject, suitable for the amateur. In 1871, when Clerk Maxwell, the first Professor of Experimental Physics in this University, gave his Intro-ductory Lecture, he had some appreciative things to say about history. He said: 'though some of us may, I hope, see reason to make the pursuit of science the main aim of our lives, it must be one of our most constant aims to main-tain a living connexion between our work and the other liberal studies of Cambridge, whether literary, philological, historical or philosophical', and again: 'the history of the development, whether normal or abnormal, of ideas is of all subjects that in which we, as thinking men, take the deepest interest'. He drew, however, a contrast between the 'clearer atmosphere' of the history of ideas and the 'working of those blind forces which, we are told, are operating on crowds of obscure people, shaking principalities and powers, and compelling reasonable men to bring events to pass in an order laid down by philosophers'.[1] He was referring, I suppose, rather to Buckle's 'science of history' than to the then recent work of Karl Marx or to the more subtle ideas of Seeley, who was then Regius Professor of Modern History. Clerk Maxwell regarded the natural scientist as 'in some measure disqualified' from studying 'the region of storms'.

Since his time there has been a vigorous movement of minute research which has brought the history of the natural sciences into an organic relation with the study of the sciences themselves. The results have illuminated many obscure passages in the history of technology and in general economic history. They have influenced the historians of philosophy and of thought in general. But, useful as this contribution to our historical knowledge has been, the impulse to it has come almost entirely from the side of the scientists, and it has served more than one of their own purposes. At one extreme, since we have lived in a period of rapid change and disturbance in scientific thought, there has been the desire to test the validity of ideas by tracing their development; but there has also been, at the opposite extreme, the recognition that science could not disclaim all responsibility for 'the lurid flow of terror and insane distress'. The wars and the social discontents of our scientific age have raised fundamental discussions of the social functions of science, and, in the course of these dis-

[1] *Scientific Papers*, II (1890), pp. 250-2.

cussions, wide tracts of the history of science are coming under cultivation.

It is difficult to tell how much historical study can contribute directly to the study of natural science. No doubt the clearest way of explaining the present state of knowledge often is to trace its past development step by step. Again, a review of this past development often enables a scientist to distinguish assumptions and hypotheses more clearly from ascertained results and so enables him to take turnings which his forerunners passed by. It is not clear, however, that the historical method can lead to new knowledge in anything like the same way as in the social sciences. In these there are at least parts of the subject-matter which cannot be apprehended except historically; in some at least of the non-human sciences there seem to be no such parts. The scientists, however, have asked for the collaboration of historians, and historians are already lending their skilled assistance in many directions.

This is one of many instances in which historical studies are becoming specialized according to their subject-matter, and when we look at the total effect of these changes it raises a disturbing question. Each of these special branches is an abstract kind of history; in order to concentrate on one aspect, it ignores the rest; but, if this process goes further, how much will be left of the integral history from which each of them has taken away its part? The specialists recognize that there is such a thing as general history; indeed, it is not uncommon for some writer who has given an exact and scholarly account of something in the past, to say, 'I am not a historian'. These words imply that the specialist is aware of a large background of facts contemporary with those he has studied, and that he relies for his knowledge of this background on the general historian. Historians will agree that this is a more tenable position than that of Buckle and other writers who wanted to absorb all knowledge of the past into a totalitarian history of civilization; but if general history is nothing but the context or background of the special histories, then, as the specialists multiply, it will be nothing but a constantly diminishing residue. In the end there will be nothing left of it except such oddments as cannot be studied by any rigorous method.

At present this is a remote or even an imaginary danger. There is still scope and need for general historians who bring together the conclusions of the specialists and supply all of them alike with a comprehensive view of the inter-related diversity of past times. I will even venture to say that we ought still to treat the life of each community in each period as a whole. Many historians are indeed now dissatisfied with the old way of taking political and con-stitutional history as the central thread through the diver-sity. Economic history, especially here in Cambridge, has vindicated its right to a high place; social history puts forward a strong claim. But it is in public institutions that men express their will to control events, and therefore it seems to me that historians will go wrong if they try to resolve political and constitutional history into other ele-ments, just as our practical men will go wrong if they follow the current fashion of treating 'cultural' interests and activities as if they could be altogether separated from the affairs of states. The history of institutions must be in some sense central; and in Maitland's university it is impossible to believe that it need be dull. Maitland was a historian of institutions, and even on their strictly legal side; but if ever any man had the genius for striking fire from shrivelled records, and for making its light flash to and fro between our time and the Middle Ages, it was Maitland. For my part I am content with the old principle that the first quality of the good historian is σύνεσις πολιτική, though I think these words should be translated not as 'political judgment' but as 'good sense in matters of public concern'. Their author regarded Thucydides as the greatest of historians, and Thucydides gave us, among other things, in his account of the plague at Athens, our first clinical account of an epidemic disease. Again, as we were taught by the late Professor Cornford, when he wrote so provocatively that Thucydides was *mythistoricus*, he saw these matters of public concern as pathways between the summits and the abysses of destiny, and so he was at once the scientific historian and the tragic dramatist.

This is the essential paradox of the historian's work, that he must be scrupulously true to fact and yet that his work is a work of creative, or rather of recreative, imagination. Nowadays it is more necessary than it once was to insist on fidelity to fact, for we hear very often in various forms the doctrine that the historian's work is personal, that nothing in the past will look the same to one age as it did to another, that historiography is never definitive and that every historical work is conditioned by the time when it is written. We need not hesitate to admit that the past will seem to change as we look at it afresh. It is a familiar experience that the same book seems very different when we read it at different stages of our lives, and it must needs be so with the infinite, polyglot records of the world. We may concede that every generation needs to rewrite its histories, though this doctrine seems to be most popular among those who do not burden themselves by much reading of the older histories. But we must not forget that there are such things as facts. Births, deaths and marriages, for instance, are facts. Neither birth nor death nor marriage looks the same in all respects to any of us now as it looked even a short century ago; but that does not invalidate everything that our grandparents believed about them and it does not mean that such events never occurred. Every historical character was born at a particular date, of particular parents, and we either know these facts about him or we do not. All our knowledge of the past has a hard core of facts, however much it may be concealed by the surrounding pulp of disputable interpretation. Yet it is true that even the driest historical work springs from imagination. What distinguishes history from the other human studies is that it deals with human life in time. Narrative is its characteristic instrument; there is no kind of historical method into which narrative does not enter as a component, and every good historian is something of a story-teller. Need I elaborate this when I stand here as the successor of the best of all our historical story-tellers? For you and me as for many thousands of others the Master of Trinity has shown over and over again that he is one of those who might say

> I can detach from me, commission forth
> Half of my soul, which in its pilgrimage
> O'er old unwandered waste ways of the world
> May chance upon some fragment

to which his magical art can give life and movement. And on the place of his work in the body of our historical knowledge I will say two things. First, the Master in bringing the past to life has never narrowed his vision within the utilitarian limits to which I confined my first remarks on liberal education. He has maintained the place of history among literary studies; the England he has written about has been his England, the England not only of Marlborough, but of Wordsworth. Then, secondly, by keeping all this alive he has served our practical needs better than any utilitarianism could have done. It is always so. England could scarcely have kept its heroism and its statesmanship if it had not remembered its poetry; and we may well be thankful that, besides the tempestuous times themselves, we have great historians to turn our minds back upon our inheritance.

For the awakened public interest in history we do indeed pay a price: as history flourishes, so the perversions of history flourish beside it. I need not take up your time by arguing against the heresy of the light-hearted biographers who eke out their disconnected knowledge by what seem to them harmless fictions. When it happens, as it often does, that hard facts prove their guesses to be wrong, we see how this silly temerity spoils all their work. Most harmful of all perversions at the present time is the use of narrative for purposes of propaganda. A great part of the streams of falsehood with which we have to contend consists of perverted narratives of the course of European events in the last four centuries, and no misrepresentation is harder to refute than a consecutive story cunningly made up from statements each of which is true if taken by itself.

Against all these perversions of history our protection is the principle that the true historian must be both a scholar and a thinker. He will never swerve from the disinterested search for truth, and he will apply to his evidence all the strict criteria which we have inherited from the scholars of the past, not only from historians, but from many others too. Equally he will take his place in the common life of thought, he will be aware of the questions which are asked and the methods which are applied even in studies far distant from his own. If historians do not investigate matters of general concern, false assumptions on their historical aspects pass unchallenged and in time are introduced into history with the prestige of some other study behind them. Since this is the two-sided nature of the historian's work, it follows that the highest standards of quality in historical research can best be maintained in our universities. Our historical faculties are not indeed suited for large tasks of co-operative re-search or for the publication of bulky records; these are tasks which we must leave to the state or to independent institutes rich enough to employ professional staffs. Re-search, however, is as much our own work as teaching; neither can thrive at a distance from the other; in both alike we must be at once scholars and thinkers, and in both characters the universities give us the apparatus and, what is even more important, the society which we need. We are members of *studia generalia*, in which alone all the faculties are always accessible and the thought of all the world has interpreters. We become familiar with the stan-dards of learning which have been passed down from hand to hand not only in set discourses but in the daily routine and the casual conversation of centuries.

On such an occasion as this a lecturer is permitted to speak of himself. Hitherto I have spent my working life in another university; but, even if I had been received with less than the most generous kindness which you have shown me, I could scarcely have felt that I had come to the Cambridge historical faculty as a stranger. I have been singularly fortunate in my opportunities for acquaintance among historians, and among them have been the Cam-bridge historians with whom I have worked. If I do not name them all, and I see that some of them are here, it is not for lack of heartfelt gratitude. I will mention only those whom I am bound especially to remember to-day. I first became a Fellow of All Souls College ten years after the death of Lord Acton, who had been one of its very few

Honorary Fellows. My older colleagues told me of his visits there and I learnt how the studies of Oxford had gained from the comments and advice of that great man. His election was one of the many acts of enlightened initiative by which All Souls has enriched the Oxford historical school; amongst them you will allow me now to commemorate the endowment of the chair of economic history which I have lately quitted after a twelve years' tenure. At another stage of my academic life, as I am happy now to recall, I was a Fellow of Oriel on the occasions when we elected two successive Cambridge Regius Professors as Honorary Fellows of our small and most friendly society. From Professor Bury we learnt how modestly great learning and force of intellect may be carried. Professor Trevelyan came to us doubly welcome, for in this relation to our college, as in so much else, his father had preceded him. If I had not known my predecessors in these ways I should still have felt, as I cannot but feel, much more than humility at the thought that I am to follow them here; but perhaps I could not have taken such comfort as I do from the assurance that they would wish me well in my purpose to serve our University.

Lightning Source UK Ltd.
Milton Keynes UK
UKHW010625010819
347207UK00001B/2/P